• N U M B E R L A N D •

LIFT-THE-FLAP
FIRST MATHS

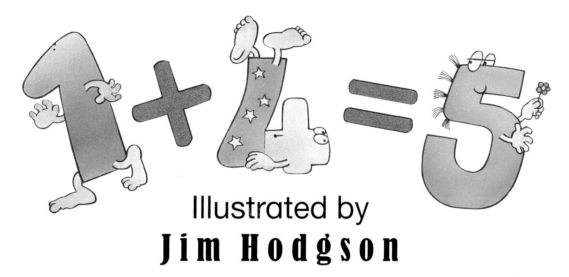

Illustrated by
Jim Hodgson

Each spread in this book deals with a different aspect of maths for young learners. By following the clear instructions that accompany each exercise, your child will be developing a sound understanding of basic mathematical concepts. But don't forget, at this age the most important thing of all is to have fun!

TEMPLAR

Introducing the NUMBERLAND characters...

Nosey Number 1

Watchful Number 2

Footsy Number 3

Starry Number 4

Hairy Number 5

Stripy Number 6

Dotty Number 7

Toothy Number 8

Spotty Number 9

Jingles Number 10

Nosey Number 1 likes having fun in the Numberland garden. Today he is playing hide-and-seek with his friends. Can you help him find them?

Who is hiding behind the tree?

The Numberland Witch needs a lot for her magic pot!

Find 1 red hen, 2 tiny mice, 3 buzzing bees, 4 sharp knives, 5 green frogs, 6 caterpillars, 7 snails, 8 magic beans, 9 little men and 10 lovely flowers.

How many brooms can you find?

$$4 + 2 = 6 \checkmark$$
$$2 + 2 = 4 \checkmark$$
$$3 + 2 = 7 \times$$
$$3 + 3 = 6 \checkmark$$

How many?

Watchful Number 2 needs some help. Can you tell him how many things there are here?

Count the butterflies.

Follow the trails.
Which snail reaches which leaf?

How many butterflies have red wings?

How many snails are there?

Give each snail one leaf. How many leaves do you have left?

This is Dilly Dragon.
She has lots of spots.

Look at this picture.

How many
blue spots?

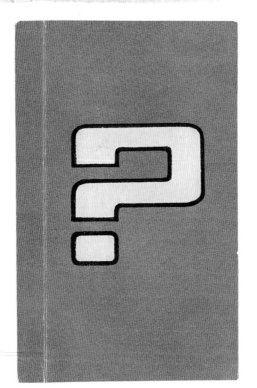

How many
green spots?

How many spots altogether?

How many
clowns?

How many
seals?

Shapes

Footsy Number 3 has a lot of shapes,
but look what a mess they are in!
Can you help to tidy them up?

Find 5 triangles. Find 4 squares.
Find 2 rectangles. Find 6 circles.

Can you find the odd ones out?

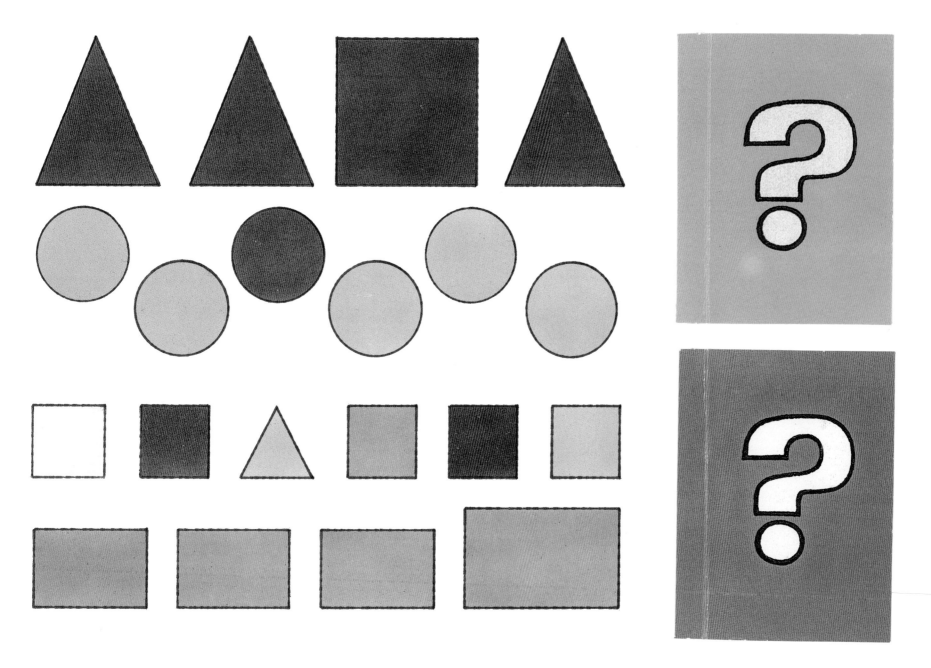

Mary Mouse is hungry! Can you help her find the way to her dinner?

Go in front of the tree, past three flowers, over four flower pots, onto the smallest bucket, under the biggest ball, up the middle-sized ladder and you will find Mary's dinner.

What would you like to eat best?

Adding Up

Starry Number 4 is learning to add up. Can you help him do these sums?

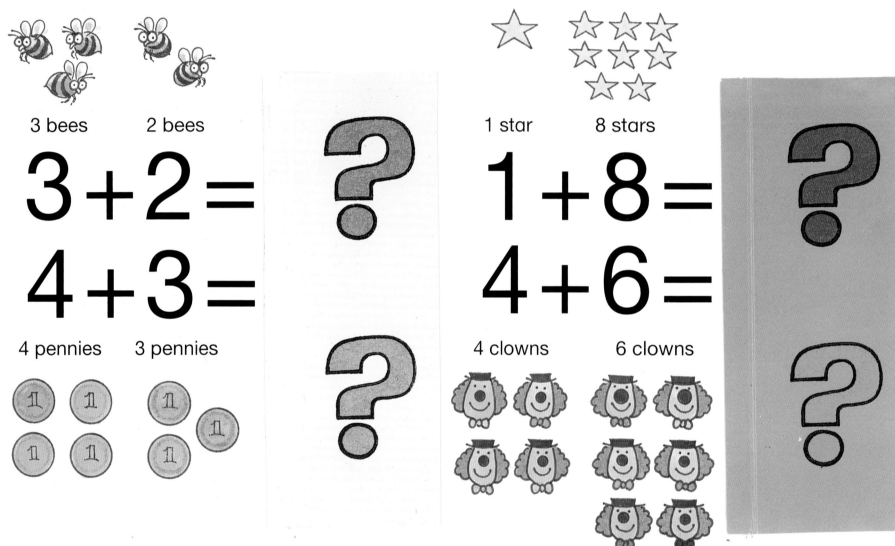

3 bees   2 bees

$3 + 2 =$

$4 + 3 =$

4 pennies   3 pennies

1 star   8 stars

$1 + 8 =$

$4 + 6 =$

4 clowns   6 clowns

1 2 3 4 5 6 7 8 9 10

Can you help Starry count his toys?
He wants to do some sums to find out how many
of each toy he has got. Please help!

3 soldiers

4 soldiers

2 bears

2 bears

4 dolls

1 doll

Bigger...

Bertie Bear and his big sister Belinda are on holiday. But at the hotel their luggage has got mixed up.

Can you help them to sort it out?

Whose sunhat is bigger?
Whose t-shirt is smaller?
Whose sandals are wider?
Whose trunks have more spots?

...Biggest!

Hairy Number 5 keeps
the Numberland records.

Find the fattest frog.
Find the longest snake.
Find the tallest bird.
Find the smallest butterfly.
Find the flower with the
most bees.

Jim and Jam, the monkey brothers, are going to the fair. They have 5p each. Jim has a go on the hoopla and the lucky dip. Jam has a go at throwing the sponge and the raffle. How much do they each have left to spend on sweets?

Pretend you have 5p. How will you spend it?

Taking Away

Stripy Number 6 has been robbed!
Look at the pictures of his room before and after the robbery.
The robber took 2 balls away. Can you find 8 other things that he took?

The farmer has lost three sheep. How many are left?

6 - 3 =

6 sheep   3 sheep

The butcher has lost four sausages. How many are left?

7 - 4 =

7 sausages   4 sausages

The baker has lost five doughnuts. How many are left?

10 - 5 =

10 doughnuts 5 doughnuts

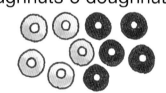

The greengrocer has lost five bananas. How many are left?

5 - 5 =

5 bananas   5 bananas

Patterns

Dotty Number 7 asked the Numberland gnomes to paint a pattern on the wall of his house, but those lazy gnomes didn't finish their patterns. Can you tell Dotty what he needs to paint?

Which animal comes next?

Which object comes next?

It's the Numberland teddy bears' picnic!

How many families of bears
can you find?
How many bears are there in all?
How many other groups of things
can you find?

Multiplying

Pat Pig is always boasting. Whenever Mary Mouse says how many things she has got, Pat Pig says he has got twice as many. Just listen to him!

I've got 1 house

I've got 2 houses

I've got 2 cats

I've got 4 cats

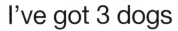

I've got 3 dogs

I've got 6 dogs.

I've got 4 fish

How many fish has Pat got?

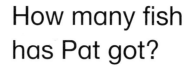

Sorting and...

Spotty Number 9 has to sort out these cats into groups.

Can you help?

Look at these bees.

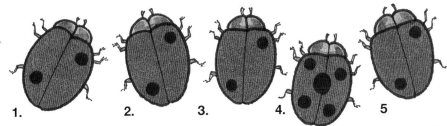

1.   2.   3.   4.

1.   2.   3.   4.   5.

Look at these ladybirds.

1.   2.   3.   4.   5

How many cats belong to the group with striped tails?

How many cats belong to the group with black ears?

Which ladybird is the odd one out?

Which bee is the odd one out?

Toothy Number 8 has been having a nightmare! What do you think he has been dreaming about?

$2 \times 2 =$

2 lots of 2 long ears

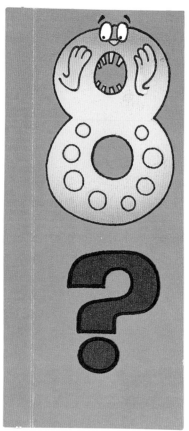

$4 \times 2 =$

4 lots of 2 big feet

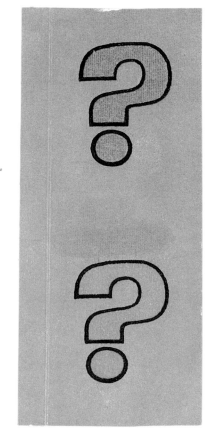

$3 \times 3 =$

3 lots of 3 spots

$2 \times 3 =$

2 lots of 3 eyes

...Matching

Dotty Number 7 has to match up these objects. Can you help?

1.
2.
3.
4.
5.
6.
7.
8.

Dotty has to guess what matches up with these two objects. Do you know?

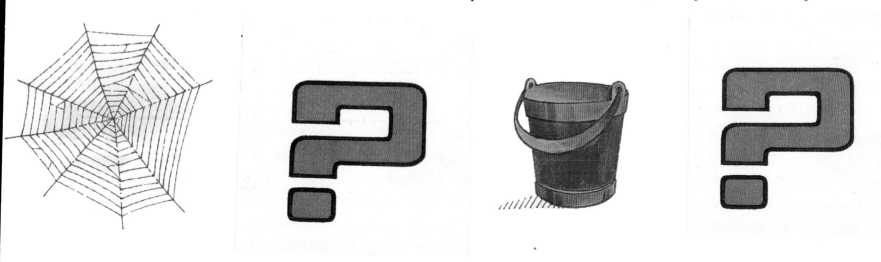

Sharing

Jingles Number 10 has made 10 delicious cakes. Help him share them out among his friends. Give each animal one cake. Do you have any left over?

Look under the flap and see!